D1372071

GREEN BAY
PACKERS

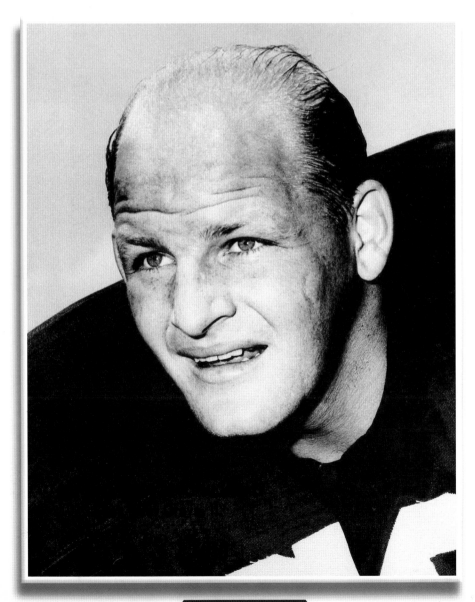

by Rob Reischel

Published by ABDO Publishing Company, 8000 West 78th Street, Edina, Minnesota 55439. Copyright © 2011 by Abdo Consulting Group, Inc. International copyrights reserved in all countries. No part of this book may be reproduced in any form without written permission from the publisher. SportsZone™ is a trademark and logo of ABDO Publishing Company.

Printed in the United States of America,
North Mankato, Minnesota
062010
092010

 THIS BOOK CONTAINS AT LEAST 10% RECYCLED MATERIALS.

Editor: Matt Tustison
Copy Editor: Nicholas Cafarelli
Interior Design and Production: Christa Schneider
Cover Design: Craig Hinton

Photo Credits: David Stluka/AP Images, cover, 4; AP Images, title page, 10, 13, 15, 17, 18, 21, 25, 28, 42 (top, middle, bottom); NFL Photos/AP Images, 7, 23, 26, 33, 34, 44; Doug Mills/AP Images, 9; Bill Haber/AP Images, 31; Roberto Borea/AP Images, 37, 43 (top); Amy Sancetta/AP Images, 39, 43 (middle); David Drapkin/AP Images, 41, 43 (bottom); Julia Robertson/AP Images, 47

Library of Congress Cataloging-in-Publication Data
Reischel, Rob, 1969-
  Green Bay Packers / Rob Reischel.
    p. cm. — (Inside the NFL)
  ISBN 978-1-61714-012-9
  1. Green Bay Packers (Football team)—History—Juvenile literature. I. Title.
  GV956.G7R43 2010
  796.332'640977561—dc22
                    2010016425

TABLE OF CONTENTS

CHAPTER 1

BRETT FAVRE

The pass was an absolute missile. At its highest point, it was maybe 12 feet off the ground. And it traveled more than 40 yards in the blink of an eye.

The Green Bay Packers trailed the visiting Cincinnati Bengals 23–17 on September 20, 1992. There were just 19 seconds left. Green Bay was out of time-outs and 35 yards from the end zone.

It was at that moment that quarterback Brett Favre became loved by Packers fans everywhere.

Favre had entered the game earlier in relief of the injured Don Majkowski. He called a play named "All Go." Favre dropped back. He then fired a throw down the right sideline. The ball somehow went between a pair of defenders. It was caught by wide receiver Kitrick Taylor for a touchdown. The play gave the Packers an improbable 24–23 win.

QUARTERBACK BRETT FAVRE LOOKS DOWNFIELD DURING THE PACKERS' 24–23 WIN OVER THE BENGALS ON SEPTEMBER 20, 1992. FAVRE MOVED INTO THE STARTING LINEUP THE NEXT WEEK AND STAYED THERE FOR 16 SEASONS.

Former Packers general manager Ron Wolf sent a first-round draft choice—the seventeenth overall pick in the 1992 NFL Draft—to the Atlanta Falcons to acquire quarterback Brett Favre in February 1992. Initially, Packers fans did not like the move. Favre was a second-round pick the previous year and had barely played as a rookie for the Falcons. "I don't know what people say is the best trade ever made," Wolf said. "But I've got to use the words here of [former Houston Oilers coach] Bum Phillips, and he said this about [star running back] Earl Campbell, 'I don't know if he's the best, but it won't take long to call the roll.' And that's kind of the way I feel about this. If it's not the best, it won't take long to call the roll."

Favre started the next game. He never left the lineup again during his 16 seasons in Green Bay.

"On that play, I was blocking on a guy and he just kind of stopped," former Packers left tackle Ken Ruettgers said. "That usually means he's given up because the ball is in the air.

"So I looked up and saw the ball just zipping down the field to Kitrick Taylor. I mean, it was an NFL Films moment. It was one of the few great moments that as a lineman you not only played, but got to witness at the same time. It was incredible."

It was also the start of perhaps the greatest Packers career. Considering that the team's storied history goes back to the first days of the National Football League (NFL), that is saying something.

Favre's Green Bay career ran from 1992 to 2007. He helped turn the Packers from an NFL laughingstock into one of the league's top teams.

"I shudder to think where we would have been without [Favre]," said former Green Bay general manager Ron Wolf, who traded for Favre in 1992. When

BRETT FAVRE PLAYED ONE SEASON WITH THE FALCONS, AS A ROOKIE IN 1991. THEY THEN TRADED HIM TO THE PACKERS.

Favre arrived in Green Bay, the Packers had been to just one playoff game in the previous 24 years. By the time he was finished, Favre led Green Bay to 22 postseason games, one Super Bowl title, and two National Football Conference (NFC) championships.

It is one of the reasons he started 275 games in a row (including the playoffs) as a Packer.

When Favre was traded from Green Bay during the summer of 2008, he left with almost every passing record in team history. Among the categories in which Favre ranks first are touchdown passes (442) and passing yards (61,655).

More importantly, the Packers went 172–103 (including playoff games) during Favre's time with the team. In his 16 seasons with Green Bay, there was only one year in which the Packers had a losing record.

Favre's place in Green Bay history is secure. But he is not the team's only legend. The Packers have had many since they first began playing in 1919.

Favre was also the first player in NFL history to win three consecutive Most Valuable Player (MVP) awards. He was named to nine Pro Bowls as a Packer. He was a first- or second-team All-Pro selection six times.

Favre cared about winning as much as any player in football.

BRETT FAVRE CELEBRATES DURING SUPER BOWL XXXI IN JANUARY 1997. GREEN BAY BEAT NEW ENGLAND 35–21 FOR ITS FIRST NFL TITLE IN 29 YEARS.

BRETT FAVRE

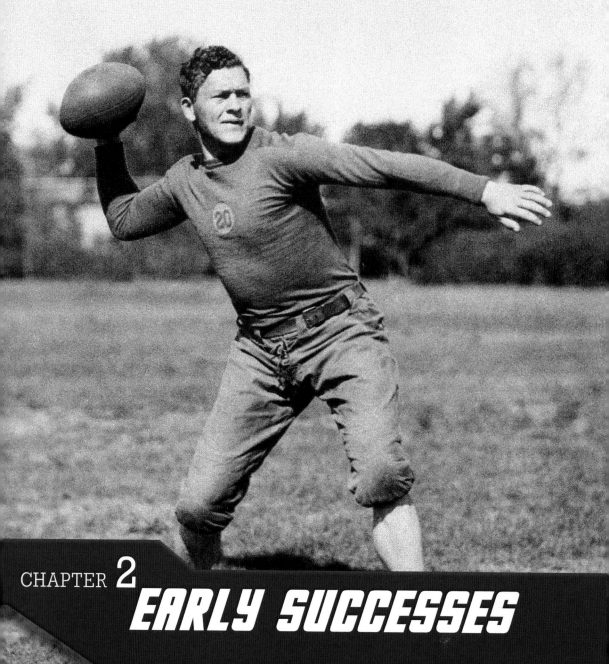

CHAPTER 2

EARLY SUCCESSES

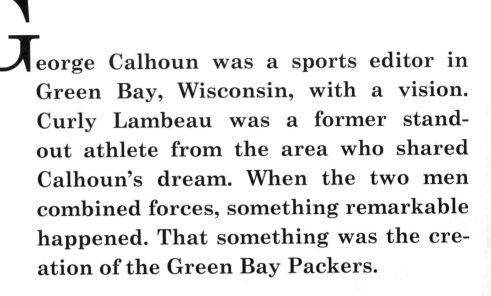

George Calhoun was a sports editor in Green Bay, Wisconsin, with a vision. Curly Lambeau was a former stand-out athlete from the area who shared Calhoun's dream. When the two men combined forces, something remarkable happened. That something was the creation of the Green Bay Packers.

Back in 1919, Calhoun was the sports editor at the *Green Bay Press-Gazette*. One day, Calhoun bumped into Lambeau. Calhoun had covered Lambeau when he was a star athlete at Green Bay East High School.

The two men talked about starting up a football team.

Calhoun ran a story asking local athletes to try out for the team. On August 11, 1919, the group of potential players met in the *Press-Gazette*'s editorial room. A football team was organized.

Shortly thereafter, Lambeau's employer—the Indian Packing Company—agreed to

CURLY LAMBEAU HELPED FOUND THE PACKERS. HE PLAYED FOR THEM FROM 1919 UNTIL 1929 AND ALSO WAS THEIR COACH FROM 1919 TO 1949.

put up the $500 needed for blue and gold uniforms. The company also allowed the team to practice on company grounds. Naturally, the nickname "Packers" developed.

That modest beginning started an amazing relationship between Lambeau and the Packers. The 21-year-old Lambeau became player-coach when Green Bay competed in its first game against the Menominee North End A. C. in 1919. He would play halfback for 11 seasons with the Packers. As was common during that era, he would sometimes take the snap and throw the ball. It was not until 1949 that he stepped down as the team's coach.

The Packers won almost as soon as Lambeau got them started. In 1919, Green Bay went 10–1 playing nonleague games against teams throughout

HEAD COACHES

As of 2010, the Packers had 14 head coaches in their storied history. It all began with Curly Lambeau. He coached Green Bay from 1921, the team's first official season, through 1949. Vince Lombardi coached the Packers from 1959 to 1967. Among Green Bay coaches, his winning percentage in the regular season and the postseason are the highest. Lombardi went 89–29–4 (.754) in the regular season and 9–1 (.900) in the playoffs. Lambeau was the team's coach longer than anyone else—for 29 years. He went 209–104–21 (.668) in the regular season. Ray (Scooter) McLean (1–10–1, .091) and Gene Ronzani (14–31–1, .311) have the lowest winning percentages in team history.

Wisconsin and Upper Michigan. Lambeau led an offense that loved to throw the ball. Most football teams during that era ran the ball far more often than they passed it.

The Packers played their games at Hagemeister Park. It was next to Green Bay East High School. The Packers did not charge for games at the time.

THE PACKERS STOP GIANTS BALL CARRIER BENNY FRIEDMAN IN A 20–6
WIN FOR GREEN BAY ON NOVEMBER 24, 1929, IN NEW YORK.

Instead, they made money by taking donations from fans.

By 1921, the Packers had become so successful that Lambeau received the backing of two officials at the packing plant. The plant had been bought out by the Acme Packing Company. The officials purchased a team in the American Professional Football Association (APFA). The APFA later became the NFL.

Calhoun worked as the team manager, publicist, and traveling secretary from 1919 to 1947. He wrote about the team in the *Press-Gazette* as well.

Andrew B. Turnbull was the *Press-Gazette*'s general manager and the Packers' president from 1923 to 1927. Turnbull helped keep the Packers alive in 1922. Financial problems affected the team that year. Then, in 1923,

Turnbull convinced local businessmen to purchase stock in the team and turn it into a nonprofit corporation. The Packers remain that way today.

From those modest roots came the team with the most NFL titles. Through the 2009 season, the Packers had won 12 league championships. The Chicago Bears ranked next with nine.

The 1929 team was Green Bay's first championship squad. The Packers went 12–0–1 and outscored their opponents 198–22. They had eight shutouts. By finishing with the best winning percentage in the NFL that season, Green Bay was declared the league's champion.

Green Bay repeated as league champion in 1930. The Packers went 10–3–1 for a .769 winning percentage. The New York Giants were 13–4 (.765) that season. Green Bay made it three titles in a row in 1931. The Packers went 12–2 and edged the Portsmouth Spartans (11–3) for the title. Green Bay's Johnny McNally had 11 receiving touchdowns and 14 total scores.

JOHNNY "BLOOD" MCNALLY

Star halfback Johnny "Blood" McNally played for the Packers from 1929 through 1933 and then again from 1935 to 1936. McNally was a native of New Richmond, Wisconsin. He was a member of four NFL championship teams with the Packers. McNally was known for his speed, agility, and pass-catching ability. Legend has it that he received the nickname "Blood" while in college at Saint John's in Collegeville, Minnesota. While passing by a movie theater, McNally saw the title of the film "Blood and Sand" on the marquee. He turned to his friend and said, "That's it. You be Sand. I'll be Blood." McNally was enshrined in the Pro Football Hall of Fame in 1963.

PACKERS WIDE RECEIVER DON HUTSON, SHOWN IN 1943, WAS NAMED THE NFL'S MVP IN 1941 AND 1942.

The Packers would have won a fourth straight title in 1932. But there was an NFL rule that said ties did not count in the standings. Green Bay finished that year 10–3–1 (.769). Chicago was 7–1–6 (.875). Under modern rules, ties are treated as a half-win and half-loss. So, today, the Packers would have had a .750 winning percentage compared to the Bears' .714.

The NFL began playing an official championship game starting with the 1933 season. The league split the teams into Eastern and Western divisions. Each division's winner would get a spot in the league title game.

The 1936 Packers won the Western Division with a 10–1–1 record. They received their first berth in the NFL Championship Game. In the contest, Green Bay star wide receiver Don Hutson caught an early 48-yard touchdown pass from quarterback Arnie Herber. The Packers beat the Boston Redskins 21–6 at the Polo Grounds in New York.

In the 1939 NFL title game, the Packers beat the Giants 27–0 at State Fair Park in Milwaukee. Green Bay's sixth and final title under Lambeau came in 1944.

DON HUTSON

Roughly once a generation, a player comes along who revolutionizes a position. In the 1930s, that man was Don Hutson. Hutson was a dynamic wide receiver for the Packers from 1935 to 1945. He set 18 NFL receiving records in his career. Amazingly, considering how teams pass the ball much more often these days, 10 of those records were still standing when Hutson died in 1997. Sports Illustrated NFL writer Peter King once called Hutson the greatest player in league history. Many still consider Hutson the greatest Packer of all time. Hutson also is often referred to as the NFL's first star wide receiver. As of 2010, among the NFL records he still held were most seasons leading the league in receptions (eight) and most seasons leading the league in receiving yards.

THE PACKERS CELEBRATE THEIR 1944 NFL TITLE. AMONG THOSE SHOWN
ARE FULLBACK TED FRITSCH (64) AND COACH CURLY LAMBEAU, WITH HAT.

Fullback Ted Fritsch scored two touchdowns (one rushing, one receiving) in the Packers' 14–7 win over the Giants at the Polo Grounds.

Green Bay has a population of only about 100,000. The Packers continue to succeed in the NFL despite playing in the league's smallest market. The Packers remain one of professional sports' most unique stories because they operate without an owner. Instead, 112,120 stockholders own 4,750,937 shares of the team. None receive a dividend on those shares.

"There aren't a whole lot of stories in sports better than that one," former Packers general manager Ron Wolf said. "If there are, I can't think of them."

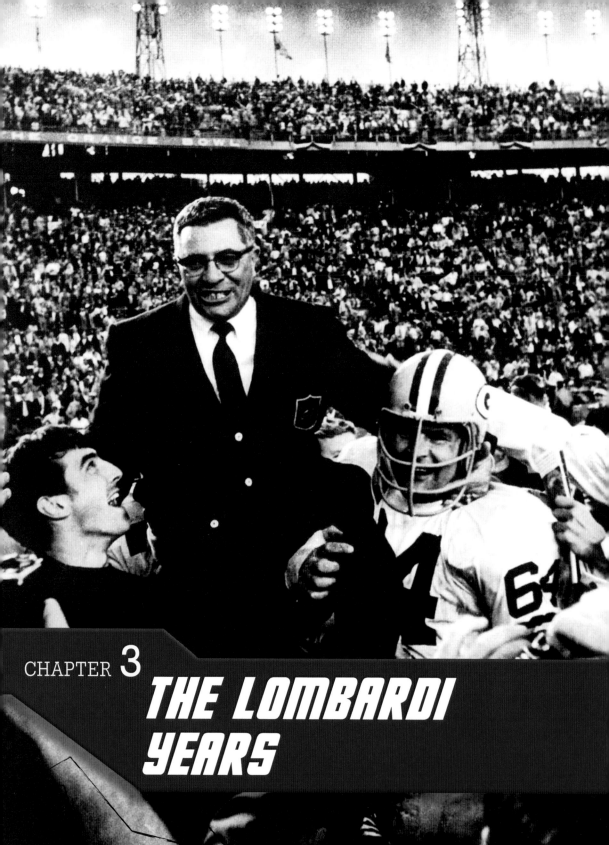

CHAPTER 3

THE LOMBARDI YEARS

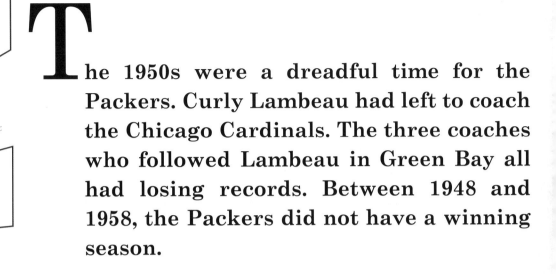

T he 1950s were a dreadful time for the Packers. Curly Lambeau had left to coach the Chicago Cardinals. The three coaches who followed Lambeau in Green Bay all had losing records. Between 1948 and 1958, the Packers did not have a winning season.

But things turned around in a big way in 1959. The Packers made the surprising move of hiring little-known Vince Lombardi as their head coach and general manager. Over the next nine seasons, the Packers were amazingly successful. They enjoyed accomplishments that the NFL has not seen since.

Lombardi had never been a head coach when he arrived in Green Bay. He had been an assistant coach, specializing in offense, with the New York Giants from 1954 to 1958. But it quickly became apparent that he was the perfect man to lead the Packers.

COACH VINCE LOMBARDI IS CARRIED OFF THE FIELD AFTER THE PACKERS DEFEATED THE RAIDERS 33–14 IN SUPER BOWL II ON JANUARY 14, 1968.

Lombardi demanded discipline, focus, and, ultimately, perfection. He changed the Packers' attitudes.

Lombardi led the Packers to their first winning season in 12 years during the 1959 campaign. By 1960, Lombardi had guided Green Bay to the NFL Championship Game. The host Philadelphia Eagles beat the Packers 17–13. But Green Bay made amends the next year. The Packers defeated Lombardi's old Giants team 37–0 in Green Bay for the title.

In 1962, Green Bay went 13–1 and captured another NFL championship. The Packers toppled the host Giants 16–7 for the title.

After a two-year drought, the Packers won three straight NFL championships between 1965 and 1967. Included in that stretch were victories in the first two Super Bowls, after the 1966 and 1967 seasons.

From 1959 to 1967, Lombardi led Green Bay to five league championships. He compiled an 89–29–4 regular-season record (.754) and went 9–1 in the playoffs (.900).

Today, the Super Bowl trophy is named after Lombardi.

FANS IN GREEN BAY CELEBRATE, INCLUDING BY HANGING FROM THE GOAL POSTS, AFTER THE PACKERS' 1961 NFL TITLE GAME WIN.

"He was the best coach ever, and I think few would question or argue that," said Jerry Kramer, a Packers guard from 1958 to 1968.

There were many talented players for the Packers during the Lombardi era. One of the key cogs was offensive tackle Forrest Gregg. Gregg was named

RAY NITSCHKE

Ray Nitschke was one of the most ferocious middle linebackers in NFL history. He played his entire career with the Packers, from 1958 to 1972. With a toothless, prison-yard look to him, Nitschke was dubbed "The Animal." It is doubtful that many creatures of the wild would have wanted to battle him. " He could put the fear of God into people," former Packers quarterback Bart Starr said. Nitschke was inducted into the Pro Football Hall of Fame in 1978.

SUPER BOWL

The Super Bowl was created as part of the agreement in 1966 between the NFL and the American Football League (AFL) to form one league. The AFL–NFL merger would not happen until 1970. In the meantime, a game was created that pitted the AFL champion against the NFL champion. It was the "Super Bowl."

The Packers won the first two Super Bowls. They routed the Kansas City Chiefs 35–10 in January 1967 and the Oakland Raiders 33–14 in January 1968. Against the Chiefs, veteran Packers wide receiver Max McGee had the game of his career. He finished with seven catches for 138 yards and two touchdowns.

In 1970, the Packers and 12 other NFL teams joined the National Football Conference (NFC). All 10 AFL teams, plus three from the NFL, formed the American Football Conference (AFC). Ever since, the NFC and AFC champions have met in the Super Bowl.

All-Pro eight times during his 14-season career in Green Bay, between 1956 and 1970. Lombardi once called him "the finest player I ever coached."

As of 2010, 10 players from the Lombardi era were Hall of Famers based on their play with Green Bay: cornerback Herb Adderley (a Packer from 1961 to 1969), defensive end Willie Davis (1960–69), Gregg, running back Paul Hornung (1957–62, 1964–66), defensive tackle Henry Jordan (1959–69), linebacker Ray Nitschke (1958–72), center Jim Ringo (1953–63), quarterback Bart Starr (1956–71), fullback Jim Taylor (1958–66), and safety Willie Wood (1960–71).

Undoubtedly, the most memorable game of Lombardi's time with Green Bay came on December 31, 1967. That frigid day, the Packers defeated the

MAX MCGEE MAKES ONE OF HIS TWO TOUCHDOWN CATCHES DURING
GREEN BAY'S 35–10 ROUT OF KANSAS CITY IN SUPER BOWL I.

visiting Dallas Cowboys 21–17 for the NFL title in a game later called "The Ice Bowl."

The temperature at kickoff was 13 below zero. The wind-chill factor dipped to minus 48. Throughout the game at Lambeau Field, it only got worse.

The contest became one of the most unforgettable in league

history. Starr scored from 1 yard out with just 13 seconds left. The touchdown gave the Packers their third straight NFL title.

Things were not always perfect with Lombardi. He was a tough coach for whom to play. But years later, his players all realized that Lombardi made them better players and men.

"He altered my life dramatically, and for the better," said Bob Long, a Packers wide receiver from 1964 to 1967. "He changed my football life and my business life, and I learned a lot from him. I learned to be mentally disciplined. I learned that in business, everything needs to be done correctly."

Lombardi coached the Packers through the 1967 season. He then stepped down and focused entirely on his job as the team's general manager.

In 1969, Lombardi decided to accept a new challenge as coach of the Washington Redskins. He turned the team around. The Redskins broke a string of 13 straight seasons without a winning record.

Then, Lombardi was diagnosed with cancer in June 1970. The cancer spread quickly. Lombardi died on September 3 of that year at the age of 57.

QUARTERBACK BART STARR (15) SNEAKS IN FOR THE WINNING TOUCHDOWN
IN GREEN BAY'S 21–17 VICTORY OVER DALLAS IN "THE ICE BOWL."

Lombardi left behind a remarkable legacy. He helped solidify Green Bay's image as "Titletown USA." That is the nickname given to the city because of the Packers' success.

JIM TAYLOR

Jim Taylor was not the fastest or strongest offensive back. But he might have been the toughest. Taylor was a Packers standout from 1958 to 1966. He ran for 1,000 yards five straight years (1960–64). Taylor and Paul Hornung formed a strong backfield tandem for the Packers in the late 1950s and early 1960s.

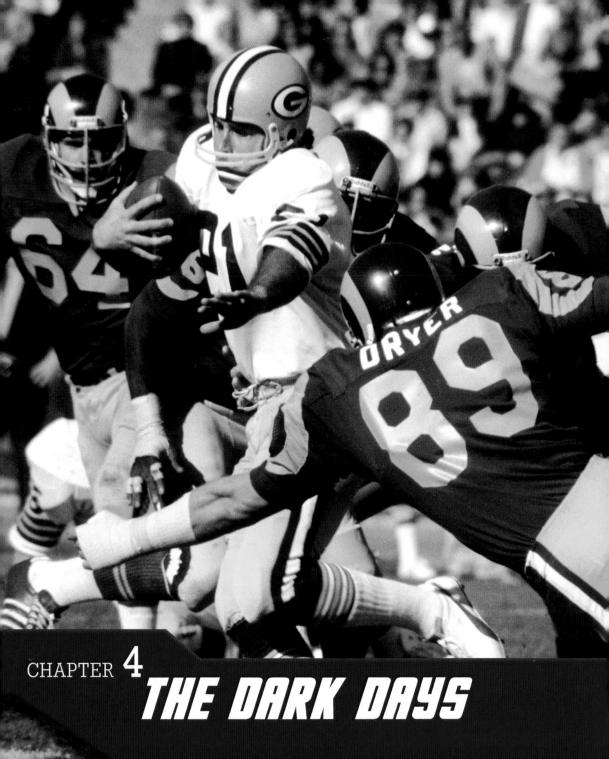

CHAPTER 4

THE DARK DAYS

Championships had become a way of life in tiny Green Bay, Wisconsin. Under coaches Curly Lambeau and Vince Lombardi, the Packers won 11 NFL titles between the 1929 and 1967 seasons. Then, the team suffered through a long period of poor play.

Between 1968 and 1991, Green Bay had just five winning seasons. The Packers reached the playoffs only twice and won only one postseason game.

Phil Bengtson was the first who tried and failed at filling Lombardi's shoes. He succeeded Lombardi as coach in 1968. Bengtson had been Lombardi's defensive coordinator. He compiled a 20–21–1 record as coach and stepped down after the 1970 season.

"Guys who were at their peak kind of started on their downside when Bengtson took over," former Packers linebacker Jim Flanigan said. "And it was kind of a no-win for Phil. Had

PACKERS QUARTERBACK JOHN HADL IS CHASED BY RAMS DEFENSIVE END FRED DRYER IN DECEMBER 1975. THE 1970s WERE DIFFICULT YEARS FOR GREEN BAY.

QUARTERBACK BART STARR AND COACH DAN DEVINE TALK IN 1971.
DEVINE HAD AN UP-AND-DOWN FOUR-SEASON TENURE WITH THE PACKERS.

he won, people would have said he was winning with Lombardi's guys. When he didn't win, he was cast as the villain. Lombardi definitely got out at the right time."

Next up was Dan Devine. He came to Green Bay from the University of Missouri. He had been the Tigers' football coach and athletic director. Devine coached the Packers from 1971 to 1974. He went 25–27–4 in that time and led the Packers to an NFC Central Division title in 1972.

Devine made a series of roster moves that set the Packers

back nearly a decade. The most significant was his trade during the 1974 season with the Los Angeles Rams for aging quarterback John Hadl. Green Bay gave up five early-round draft picks to acquire Hadl. He played just a season and a half for the Packers and did not perform well.

"I mean, history will show Dan Devine tore that team up and he tore up that franchise," former Green Bay wide receiver Barry Smith said. ". . . Let's face it. That's what he did."

Bart Starr could not duplicate his success as a player when he took over as the Packers' coach and general manager. Between 1975 and 1983, Green Bay went 52–76–3 under Starr. The Packers qualified for the playoffs just once.

"Going back to coach in Green Bay was the biggest mistake I ever made," Starr said. "I was approached by the organization, and it turned out to be an enormous mistake. I was extremely disappointed. I disappointed the Packers and their fans."

In Starr's defense, he inherited a mediocre roster of players. Devine's trade for Hadl did not give Starr a chance to add much

JAMES LOFTON

One of the bright spots for Green Bay in the late 1970s through the mid-1980s was the play of wide receiver James Lofton.

The Packers drafted Lofton in the first round, sixth overall, out of Stanford University in 1978. Lofton had 50 or more catches in seven of his nine seasons with Green Bay and reached 1,000 receiving yards in five seasons. He finished his Packers career with 530 receptions for 9,656 yards (still a team record through 2009) and 49 touchdowns. The speedy and athletic Lofton was selected to seven Pro Bowls while with Green Bay.

Lofton went on to play for four other teams. He enjoyed his greatest post-Packers success with the Buffalo Bills. Lofton retired after the 1993 season and was enshrined in the Pro Football Hall of Fame in 2003.

young talent. Green Bay did begin to show some signs of life under Starr. The Packers went 21–19–1 in his final three years and qualified for the postseason in the strike-shortened 1982 season. The Packers defeated the visiting St. Louis Cardinals 41–16 in a wild-card playoff game. But Green Bay lost 37–26 to the host Dallas Cowboys in the next round. It was Starr's last playoff game as the Packers' coach.

"Early on, my inexperience hurt us, but in the later years, we had some good draft choices and we were beginning to make progress," Starr said. "But I don't want it to sound like I'm making excuses. I just didn't get it done."

The Packers tried turning back the clock again. They replaced Starr in 1984 with Forrest Gregg. Gregg had been

JAMES LOFTON MAKES A 6-YARD TOUCHDOWN RECEPTION IN THE PACKERS' 37–26 PLAYOFF LOSS TO THE COWBOYS IN JANUARY 1983.

one of the finest offensive linemen in team history. But his coaching tenure was an even bigger disaster than Starr's.

Gregg went just 25–37–1 in his four seasons as coach. He certainly did not make many friends in his return to Green Bay.

"Bart and Forrest were like night and day," former Packers quarterback Lynn Dickey said. "Bart would work you extremely hard physically. I've never worked harder than I did under Bart. But he treated people with decency and treated you like a man.

"Forrest came in, and he yelled at you and he insulted you in front of the team. Some things went on with him that would never work at any level. Forrest knew his Xs and Os, but he had no idea about people skills. . . . It was a bad situation."

Things got better—but only slightly—under Lindy Infante. He coached the team from 1988 to 1991. The Packers were 10–6 in a memorable 1989 campaign. Third-year quarterback Don Majkowski emerged with a standout season. Majkowski was nicknamed the "Majik Man." Second-year player Sterling Sharpe became Majkowski's go-to receiver.

Infante went just 24–40 and was fired after four seasons. "It's not a pleasant thing to go through," Infante said of his firing. "I gave my absolute best. I can live with that. . . . I'm not an excuse maker."

GREEN BAY'S DON MAJKOWSKI, *RIGHT*, AND STERLING SHARPE CHAT IN 1989. MAJKOWSKI THREW 27 TOUCHDOWN PASSES, 12 TO SHARPE, THAT SEASON.

CHAPTER 5

RETURN TO GLORY

After nearly three decades of rough times, the Packers and their faithful were starved for success. Finally, "Packer Nation" feasted during the 1996 season.

Green Bay defeated the New England Patriots 35–21 in Super Bowl XXXI on January 26, 1997, at the Superdome in New Orleans, Louisiana. The win capped the most magical of seasons. The Packers earned their first NFL title in 29 years.

Brett Favre threw for 246 yards and two touchdowns with no interceptions. One of the touchdown tosses went for 81 yards to Antonio Freeman. The other was a 54-yard strike to Andre Rison. Favre also ran for a 2-yard touchdown. Green Bay's lead was trimmed to 27–21 in the third quarter. But Desmond Howard returned the following kickoff 99 yards for a touchdown. The score gave the Packers some welcome breathing room. Defensive end Reggie White also had a big game with three sacks.

DEFENSIVE END REGGIE WHITE HOISTS THE VINCE LOMBARDI TROPHY AFTER THE PACKERS WON SUPER BOWL XXXI ON JANUARY 26, 1997.

STERLING SHARPE

Wide receiver Sterling Sharpe played for the Packers from 1988 to 1994. His career was cut short because of a neck injury. But he helped the Packers become a winning team again.

Green Bay selected Sharpe in the first round, seventh overall, out of the University of South Carolina in 1988. He set a Packers rookie record with 55 receptions in 1988, and he only got better. In his second season, Sharpe had 90 catches to lead the NFL. He became the first Packer to top the league in that category since Don Hutson in 1945.

Through 2009, Sharpe held Green Bay records for touchdown catches in a season (18 in 1994), receptions in a season (112 in 1993), and consecutive games catching a pass (103, from 1988 to 1994).

Sharpe's younger brother Shannon was a star tight end with the Denver Broncos and Baltimore Ravens from 1990 to 2003.

Green Bay held on, and the celebration began.

"The biggest thing I remember was holding that trophy up and seeing [Vince] Lombardi's name," former Packers safety LeRoy Butler said. "It brought a tear to my eye because we said the trophy was coming back home."

The Packers' Super Bowl-winning pinnacle can be traced to four critical steps.

First, the team named Ron Wolf general manager on November 27, 1991. Wolf had worked in the front offices of the Oakland/Los Angeles Raiders and Tampa Bay Buccaneers. Wolf then quickly fired coach Lindy Infante and replaced him with Mike Holmgren. Holmgren had achieved great success as the San Francisco 49ers' offensive coordinator.

COACH MIKE HOLMGREN REACTS IN DECEMBER 1993 AFTER THE PACKERS EARNED THEIR FIRST PLAYOFF SPOT IN A NONSTRIKE SEASON SINCE 1972.

On February 10, 1992, Wolf traded with the Atlanta Falcons for Favre. Favre would go on to establish himself as the finest player in team history. And White, who had been a star with the Philadelphia Eagles, signed a free-agent contract with the Packers on April 8, 1993.

The quartet of Wolf, Holmgren, Favre, and White led the Packers' rebirth. They helped turn the organization from a league-wide laughingstock into a Super Bowl champion.

"What we did up there defies description," Wolf said. "No one thought the Green Bay Packers could win again."

The Packers did not just win. They won big. Holmgren led Green Bay to the postseason during his second and third seasons. Then, the 1995 Packers reached the NFC Championship Game. By the start of the 1996 season, the Packers expected a Super Bowl run. They delivered.

LEROY BUTLER

Quarterback Brett Favre and defensive end Reggie White are usually recognized as Green Bay's best players of the past two decades. But LeRoy Butler holds a special place in fans' hearts. Butler was arguably the most dynamic safety in team history, finishing with 38 interceptions. He played his entire career with Green Bay, from 1990 to 2001. Butler was named to four Pro Bowls and selected to the NFL 1990s All-Decade Team. "My game was always positive and about being a leader," Butler said. "And people always associated me with trying to win, thanking the fans for spending their hard-earned money to come and see us play, the Lambeau Leap. Stuff like that."

That year, Green Bay ranked first in the NFL in total offense and total defense. The Packers dominated their opponents by a combined score of 456–210.

The Packers hosted and defeated San Francisco and the Carolina Panthers in the playoffs by a total score of 65–27 to reach Super Bowl XXXI. In that game, Howard set a Super Bowl record with 244 return yards and became the first special teams player to earn MVP honors.

Green Bay went back to the Super Bowl the next season. The Packers entered Super Bowl XXXII at Qualcomm Stadium in San Diego, California, as heavy favorites over the Denver Broncos. However, the Broncos and star quarterback John Elway upset the Packers 31–24. Terrell Davis rushed for 157 yards and three touchdowns for Denver.

GREEN BAY'S DESMOND HOWARD BREAKS AWAY ON A 99-YARD KICKOFF
RETURN FOR A TOUCHDOWN IN SUPER BOWL XXXI.

Still, the reversal of fortunes in tiny Green Bay was a remarkable story.

Wolf was Green Bay's general manager for nine seasons. In that time, the Packers enjoyed plenty of success. They had seven consecutive winning seasons, from 1992 to 1998. They made six straight playoff appearances, from 1993 to 1998. They also won three NFC Central Division titles in a row, from 1995 to 1997. Last, they had a 25-game winning streak at Lambeau Field—the second-longest home winning streak in NFL history.

The Packers have stayed among the NFL's top teams since Wolf's retirement after the 2000 season.

Green Bay reached the postseason six times between 2001 and 2009 and played in the 2007 NFC Championship Game. The Packers lost 23–20 in overtime to the visiting New York Giants in that contest. General manager Ted Thompson traded Favre away after the 2007 season. Thompson turned the quarter-backing duties over to Aaron Rodgers in the most controversial move in team history.

But Rodgers began making a name for himself right away. In his first two seasons as the starter—2008 and 2009—Rodgers threw for nearly 8,500 yards and 58 touchdowns with just 20 interceptions. He also led the Packers to the 2009 postseason. In the wild-card round, Green Bay lost a memorable 51–45 overtime game to the host Arizona Cardinals. The 96 combined points set an NFL playoff record.

Rodgers reached his first Pro Bowl in 2009. He ranked fourth in the NFL in passer rating (103.2) and threw for 4,434 yards. More importantly, he led Green Bay to an 11–5 record and a postseason appearance.

Said Green Bay coach Mike McCarthy: "Aaron Rodgers is

AHMAN GREEN

The second-greatest trade of Ron Wolf's tenure as Green Bay's general manager came when he acquired running back Ahman Green from the Seattle Seahawks in 2000 for cornerback Fred Vinson. Green went on to set the Packers' career rushing record in 2009, in his second stint with the team. "I'm fortunate enough to be a part of that elite group of guys that has a chance to be in the record books for the Green Bay Packers," Green said. Green had 8,322 rushing yards with the Packers through 2009.

PACKERS QUARTERBACK AARON RODGERS LOOKS FOR AN OPEN RECEIVER.
RODGERS THREW 30 TOUCHDOWN PASSES IN 2009.

a Pro Bowl quarterback, and that's the facts. Trust me, I fully understand the greatness of Brett Favre. . . . But this is the beginning of potentially another great career at quarterback here in Green Bay, and [fans] should embrace it."

As quarterback for the team with perhaps the richest history in the NFL, Rodgers is trying to help bring meaning back to the phrase "Titletown USA."

TIMELINE

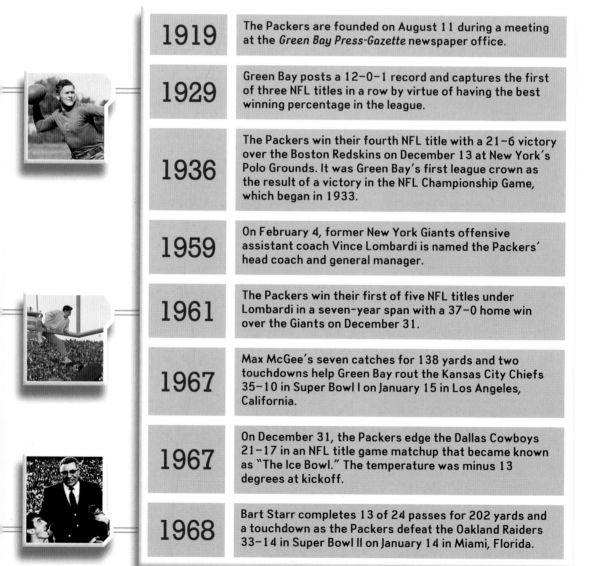

1919 — The Packers are founded on August 11 during a meeting at the *Green Bay Press-Gazette* newspaper office.

1929 — Green Bay posts a 12-0-1 record and captures the first of three NFL titles in a row by virtue of having the best winning percentage in the league.

1936 — The Packers win their fourth NFL title with a 21-6 victory over the Boston Redskins on December 13 at New York's Polo Grounds. It was Green Bay's first league crown as the result of a victory in the NFL Championship Game, which began in 1933.

1959 — On February 4, former New York Giants offensive assistant coach Vince Lombardi is named the Packers' head coach and general manager.

1961 — The Packers win their first of five NFL titles under Lombardi in a seven-year span with a 37-0 home win over the Giants on December 31.

1967 — Max McGee's seven catches for 138 yards and two touchdowns help Green Bay rout the Kansas City Chiefs 35-10 in Super Bowl I on January 15 in Los Angeles, California.

1967 — On December 31, the Packers edge the Dallas Cowboys 21-17 in an NFL title game matchup that became known as "The Ice Bowl." The temperature was minus 13 degrees at kickoff.

1968 — Bart Starr completes 13 of 24 passes for 202 yards and a touchdown as the Packers defeat the Oakland Raiders 33-14 in Super Bowl II on January 14 in Miami, Florida.

1991	On November 27, the Packers hire experienced NFL front-office man Ron Wolf as executive vice president/general manager.
1992	On January 11, Wolf hires former San Francisco 49ers offensive coordinator Mike Holmgren as coach.
1992	On February 10, Wolf trades a first-round choice, seventeenth overall, in the 1992 NFL Draft to the Atlanta Falcons for quarterback Brett Favre.
1997	On January 26, the Packers beat the New England Patriots 35–21 in Super Bowl XXXI at the Superdome in New Orleans, Louisiana. Desmond Howard returns a kickoff 99 yards for a touchdown and is selected as the game's MVP.
1998	The Denver Broncos upset the Packers 31–24 in Super Bowl XXXII at Qualcomm Stadium in San Diego, California, on January 25. Favre throws for three touchdowns.
2006	On January 12, the Packers name Mike McCarthy, who had been the 49ers' offensive coordinator, as head coach. The team had fired coach Mike Sherman 10 days earlier.
2008	Packers general manager Ted Thompson trades Favre, on August 6, to the New York Jets for a conditional pick in the 2009 NFL Draft. The selection ends up being a third-rounder.
2010	On January 10, Aaron Rodgers passes for 423 yards and four touchdowns in the Packers' 51–45 wild-card playoff loss to the host Arizona Cardinals. Arizona's Kurt Warner throws for 379 yards and five touchdowns.

QUICK STATS

FRANCHISE HISTORY
1921–

SUPER BOWLS
(wins in bold)
1966 (I), **1967 (II)**, **1996 (XXXI)**,
1997 (XXXII)

NFL CHAMPIONSHIP GAMES
(wins in bold)
1936, 1938, **1939**, **1944**, 1960, **1961**,
1962, **1965**, **1966**, **1967**

NFC CHAMPIONSHIP GAMES
(since 1970 AFL-NFL merger)
1995, 1996, 1997, 2007

DIVISION CHAMPIONSHIPS
(since 1970 AFL-NFL merger)
1972, 1995, 1996, 1997, 2002, 2003,
2004, 2007

KEY PLAYERS
(position, seasons with team)
Herb Adderley (CB, 1961–69)
Brett Favre (QB, 1992–2007)
Forrest Gregg (OT; 1956, 1958–70)
Paul Hornung (RB; 1957–62,
    1964–66)
Don Hutson (WR, 1935–45)
Johnny "Blood" McNally
    (RB; 1929–33, 1935–36)
Ray Nitschke (LB, 1958–72)
Bart Starr (QB, 1956–71)
Jim Taylor (FB, 1958–66)
Reggie White (DE, 1993–98)

KEY COACHES
Mike Holmgren (1992–98):
    75–37–0; 9–5 (playoffs)
Earl (Curly) Lambeau (1921–49):
    209–104–21; 3–2 (playoffs)
Vince Lombardi (1959–67):
    89–29–4; 9–1 (playoffs)

HOME FIELDS
Lambeau Field (1957–)
    Known as New City Stadium
    (1957–64)
    The Packers also played games in
    Milwaukee (1933–94)
City Stadium (1925–56)
Bellevue Park (1923–24)
Hagemeister Park (1921–22)

* All statistics through 2009 season

QUOTES AND ANECDOTES

"Maybe winning isn't everything, but it sure comes way ahead of whatever is second."
—Former Packers coach Vince Lombardi

For decades, the Packers played two or three regular-season home games each year in Milwaukee, Wisconsin. Most of those games were held at the State Fair Park fairgrounds and Milwaukee County Stadium. The Packers did not move their entire home schedule to Green Bay until 1995.

Until 2003, the Packers had never lost a home playoff game. They were 13–0, with 11 of the wins at Lambeau Field and two more in Milwaukee. The streak ended on January 4, 2003. The Atlanta Falcons defeated the Packers 27–7 in a wild-card game. The Packers would also lose 31–17 to the visiting Minnesota Vikings two years later in a wild-card contest.

Donald Driver holds the Packers' record for most receptions in a career. Kabeer Gbaja-Biamila is the team's all-time leader in sacks. Both players were almost afterthoughts in the NFL Draft, though. The Packers selected Driver in the seventh round in 1999, and they chose "KGB" in the fifth round in 2000.

"I really enjoyed a lot of off-the-field stuff. It kind of gave us an indication of what we were in store for at the end of the year. I just enjoyed the entire year. I enjoyed the coaches, the people, my teammates. We made the most of the opportunity. We had fun. We had fun at practice. We had fun off the field. It was a brotherhood. . . . Just the camaraderie was amazing."
—Former Green Bay running back Edgar Bennett, on the 1996 Packers' Super Bowl-winning season

GLOSSARY

All-Pro

An award given to the top players at their positions regardless of their conference. It is a high honor as there are fewer spots on the All-Pro team than on the Pro Bowl teams.

berth

A place, spot, or position, such as in the NFL playoffs.

contract

A binding agreement about, for example, years of commitment by a football player in exchange for a given salary.

draft

A system used by professional sports leagues to select new players in order to spread incoming talent among all teams.

franchise

An entire sports organization, including the players, coaches, and staff.

general manager

The executive who is in charge of the team's overall operation. He or she hires and fires coaches, drafts college players, and signs free agents.

hall of fame

A place built to honor noteworthy achievements by athletes in their respective sports.

postseason

Games played in the playoffs by the top teams after the regular-season schedule has been completed.

Pro Bowl

A game after the regular season in which the top players from the AFC play against the top players from the NFC.

retire

To officially end one's career.

rookie

A first-year professional athlete.

FOR MORE INFORMATION

Further Reading

Havel, Chris. *Favre: For the Record*. New York: Bantam Doubleday Dell Publishing Group, 1997.

Kramer, Jerry, and Dick Schapp. *Instant Replay*. New York: Doubleday, 1968.

Reischel, Rob. *Packers Essential: Everything You Need to Know to Be a Real Fan*. Chicago: Triumph Books, 2006.

Web Links

To learn more about the Green Bay Packers, visit ABDO Publishing Company online at **www.abdopublishing.com**. Web sites about the Packers are featured on our Book Links page. These links are routinely monitored and updated to provide the most current information available.

Places to Visit

Green Bay Packers Hall of Fame

1265 Lombardi Ave.
Green Bay, WI 54304
920-569-7512
www.packershalloffame.org
Nearly 80 exhibits chronicling the Packers' unique history are on display in this 25,000-square-foot area housed at Lambeau Field.

Lambeau Field

1265 Lombardi Ave.
Green Bay, WI 54304
920-569-7513
www.lambeaufield.com
This historic stadium, billed by the team as "the crown jewel of the NFL," is where the Packers play their home exhibition, regular-season, and playoff games.

Pro Football Hall of Fame

2121 George Halas Drive Northwest
Canton, OH 44708
330-456-8207
www.profootballhof.com
This hall of fame and museum highlights the greatest players and moments in the history of the National Football League. As of 2010, 26 people affiliated with the Packers were enshrined, including Curly Lambeau, Vince Lombardi, Bart Starr, and Reggie White.

INDEX

About the Author

Rob Reischel covers the Green Bay Packers for the *Milwaukee Journal Sentinel*'s Packer Plus. He has written two other books about the Packers—*Packers Essential* and *100 Things Packers Fans Should Know & Do Before They Die*. Reischel has also won several writing awards from the Wisconsin Newspaper Association. Reischel lives in Menomonee Falls, Wisconsin, with his family.